CARING FOR OLDER HORSES AND PONIES

by
Susan McBane

Illustrations by
Carole Vincer

KENILWORTH PRESS

First published in Great Britain by
Kenilworth Press Limited,
Addington, Buckingham, MK18 2JR

British Library Cataloguing in Publication Data
A catalogue record for this book is available from the British Library.

ISBN 1-872119-70-0

Printed in Great Britain by Westway Offset

The UK's **Veteran Horse Society** is dedicated to the welfare of all horses and ponies over the age of fifteen. It has a centre where horses are taken in and rehabilitated, if necessary, before being rehomed to its members. It runs a major country-wide showing series with a final at the Horse of the Year Show at Olympia.

The Veteran Horse Society
Hendre Fawr Farm
St Dogmaels
nr Cardigan
North Pembrokeshire
SA43 3LZ

tel: 01239 881300
email: geberak@veteranhorsesociety.co.uk
website: www.veteranhorsesociety.co.uk

CONTENTS

INTRODUCTION

The major advantage of domestication to horses and their owners is the continually improving health care available. When you consider that most feral horses only live to about twelve years of age and are considered very lucky to reach fifteen, you have some idea of how much longer we are now able to keep our horses going, and particularly ponies, who tend to live longer than horses.

Correct dental care is a major factor, as feral horses usually die of starvation from overgrown, uneven and sharp back teeth. If they live in areas where they are preyed upon, weakness may make them easy game for predators and they may be killed before they starve to death.

Along with dental care, we now have greatly improved knowledge of nutrition available to us, vaccinations, drugs and veterinary and complementary therapies plus management techniques to help with the debilitating diseases of old age. Domestic horses of twenty years of age were fairly rare a hundred years ago but are common now (there are always exceptions which live to great ages).

Attitudes, too, change. At one time an older horse was considered 'past it' at around fifteen to eighteen, even though still active and happy. Today, we are more willing to persevere with an older horse, to help him with management, additional therapies and veterinary techniques, rather than feel that spending money on these things is a waste of time and money.

Older horses are a double-edged sword. Their maturity and experience may have made them tolerant, caring in their own way, good at their jobs and understanding of humans (good and bad), but they can also develop some tricks of the trade, read their owner like a book, become a bit world-weary or even cynical (yes, I know we're talking horses here) and have various physical problems which may limit their performance and cost us money.

Like us, horses and ponies do change with age and life experience, and their work and care has to change accordingly if we are to enable them to continue to lead fulfilling and active lives for both our sakes.

This book is a hands-on and very practical guide to adapting to an ageing equine in the family. I hope that it will also help those taking on an older equine, particularly anyone who has not experienced equine senior citizens before.

HOW HORSES AGE

As prey animals, horses need to mature very quickly. A foal learns in twenty-four hours basically what it needs to know to survive – suckling, staying by its mother, and how to run.

By three years of age, feral horses often start their own herds and are practically mature, although they will normally put on height till about six years of age. Because life in the wild is hard, they are at their prime for only about five years, then start the downhill slide to old age, which comes at about twelve to fifteen years of age. Ponies usually live longer, partly due to their small size.

In adolescence, riding horses are worked lightly at three years of age, slightly harder progressively at four and five, and can take on almost a full workload at six. They are in their physical prime from six or seven to roughly twelve to fifteen years of age and can do their hardest work then.

Even after twelve-plus years, horses can work well, perhaps at different jobs, but when their time comes they often deteriorate quickly, in a matter of a very few years.

Picture Guide No. 15, *Mouths and Bits*, gives a good description of teeth at different ages. A simple way of telling the approximate age from the teeth is to judge the slope of the front or incisor teeth – the more V-shaped they are from the side, the older the horse. Also, a brown furrow, Galvayne's Groove, appears at the top of the outer incisor at about ten years of age and has grown out by about thirty.

Other signs are a sagging of the back and belly, legs less straight from the side than formerly, hollows above the eye, grey hairs on the head and a general lack of muscle tone, particularly along the top line.

ADOLESCENCE

PRIME TIME

OLD AGE

CHANGES IN THE BODY

Like all creatures, horses' bodies perform less efficiently as they age. Here are some of the physical changes that may be seen in middle-aged to old horses (roughly 15-25+).

Slackening muscles and other soft tissues which reduce the level of work a horse can do.
Hollows above the eyes occur: these are normally filled with fat which is used up as the horse ages, despite feeding.
Slower coat change is common in older horses and ponies. Retention of the winter coat can indicate Cushing's disease.
Reducing appetite: this may be due to ageing or dental problems and should be checked.
Changes in movement may be seen as a horse stiffens up, or old injuries or foot problems become chronic and the horse tries to adapt to them by moving in a different way (compensatory movement). Discuss the changes with your vet and farrier – don't dismiss them.
Changes in eating and drinking behaviour and digestion are common in old animals. The teeth may need attention or there may be growths in the mouth or throat making these activities difficult. The digestion will naturally deteriorate. Older horses are more prone to colic than young ones.
Changes in respiration: 'broken wind' or 'heaves' may become chronic and worsen if the animal has not been clinically treated and managed properly.
Changes in bones and feet: bones become more brittle with age and, remember, the feet also contain bones and joints. Cartilage, the 'cushion' between bone-ends, can become worn or damaged and osteoarthritis may well occur in older animals.
Changes in performance ability and attitude

to work may occur in a horse or pony who knows very well that he just can't do what he used to. This can lead to loss of performance, refusing jumps, 'bad' behaviour and failure to thrive, from stress.
General weakness and poorer bodily function result from general deterioration, all of the above conditions and others. If you have owned an animal from when it was young, you can easily overlook ageing but finally have to admit that your pride and joy is 'getting on a bit'. You can greatly help matters by **adapting fitness levels and programmes**. Most old horses with minor problems are better kept active at lower levels of demand and under veterinary supervision. Be especially careful about monitoring heart and lung fitness by frequently taking pulse and respiration levels. Hotbloods such as Thoroughbreds and Arabs and the like, frequently don't know when to stop. Don't let your horse fool you. Keep track of his heartbeat/pulse, breathing, sweating, any look of anxiety about him – and call a halt long before he does. Tiredness or lethargy the day after work are a sure sign that he – or you – have overdone things.

These pictures are slightly exaggerated but show limb changes which may occur due to slackening or damaged soft tissues (supportive ligaments mainly). The horse may appear 'over at the knee' (far left), 'back at the knee' (left) or may show dropped fetlocks (below).

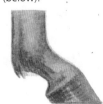

Condition scoring

This is a way of monitoring your horse's bodyweight by giving him a score, usually out of six, for his body condition, or weight. The grey areas on the five-year-old horse (top right) show the areas used for assessment, and the hindquarters diagram shows an emaciated horse 'inside' his obese alter ego.

0 = **emaciated**: virtually skin and bone

1 = **poor**: similar but not quite so marked

2 = **moderate/fair**: a little fleshy cover but ribs, backbone and hips (pelvis) easily seen

3 = **good/normal**: some topline, muscle tone, ribs, backbone and hips easily felt but not seen

4 = **fat**: neck becoming cresty, ribs, backbone and hips hard to feel, may be a 'gutter' between fat pads along backbone

5 = **obese**: hard crest with ridges of fat, 'appley' quarters, notable gutter, ribs, backbone and hips unable to be felt

Old horses, whether retired or working, should be condition scored every two weeks. Ideal, healthy condition is 3. In general, you should feed a horse of any age so that you cannot see his ribs but can feel them quite easily.

5 years

15 years

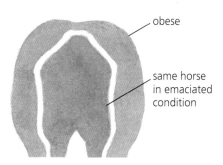

obese

same horse in emaciated condition

25 years

How old is 'old'?

It is hard to define when a horse actually becomes old but from fifteen or sixteen years onwards most insurance companies will not insure horses for disease, only injury. Biological age – the extent to which the body succumbs to ageing – varies from individual to individual and this is far more important than the horse's age in years.

It is not unusual for fifteen-year-olds to compete in three-day events, point-to-points, steeplechases and show-jumping classes. The first three demand the highest levels of athletic performance in terms of fitness and stamina, while show-jumping requires great agility and power.

Most riding schools can boast a couple of old-timer ponies, even into their thirties, who are still teaching children, because the level of their work has been sensibly reduced as they have aged. Former high-level performance horses can become valued schoolmasters and may still compete at a lower level because they have had good and fair treatment.

Dressage horses can easily compete into their late teens, while the Spanish Riding School's Lipizzaner stallions perform taxing airs well into their twenties.

So, horses can work hard to quite an advanced age **if** they are worked fairly. They also need good veterinary and management back-up. As with human athletes, those who succumb earliest to the disorders of wear and tear, in particular weakened limb soft tissues and osteoarthritis, are those who have been worked at peak level at every opportunity for as long as they could – often the most talented and able.

When fifteen-year-old steeplechasers can compete in the Grand National and give an excellent account of themselves, it makes you wonder why fifteen-year-olds are so often considered 'past it'. The age of fifteen years is no great drawback these days if a horse has been well cared for and fairly worked.

Many show jumpers are quite elderly by some standards but if they are still jumping at Grade A or above (UK) or even internationally, they must have been properly trained, worked and managed – and that makes a big difference.

AGE-RELATED PERSONALITY AND HABIT CHANGES

Animals seem to be very much like people in that many change as they get older, for better or for worse, or not at all. However, the effects of life experiences must be taken into consideration and these can certainly change people and animals in unexpected ways. A major physical or mental trauma can make humans reassess their lives, and, although we cannot know whether or not they can do that, horses are known to change after major experiences.

The great steeplechaser, Crisp, never won another major race, I understand, after he was beaten, under top weight, by the lightly handicapped Red Rum in the Grand National. It was said to have broken his heart. The then world record high-jump holder, Swank, similarly never jumped another fence, I believe, after his stupendous feat; it must just have cost too much of his spirit.

It is important to be open to personality changes with age and to adapt to a horse's new needs or wishes. The most common change, I find, in old horses is that they may become more laid-back, take life more as it comes and, physically, definitely become more susceptible to extremes of anything, particularly the weather. They also often have more time for humans if they didn't before (although there are always exceptions), become quite definite in what they like and dislike, and strict about their personal routine such as time of exercise and in which corners they want their water and hay, for instance.

It is well worthwhile acknowledging and pandering to these foibles, and it seems only fair to do so after a lifetime of service.

Older animals become much more susceptible to extremes of weather and will let us know when they need to be brought in – in which case it is only fair, and good management, to do so.

Some horses and ponies definitely make their wishes known more clearly when older – including when they want to be left in peace and quiet.

If your horse is one of those who becomes a great softy with age, it's good to be able to spend more time with him just fussing, saying thank you for everything, and reaffirming your relationship.

AGE-RELATED HEALTH CONDITIONS

Some conditions are more common in older equines than in youngsters, and the more common ones are discussed here. It is essential to call your vet whenever you note any changes in your horse's health or state of being. More than one condition may affect a horse and treatment and management for each will have to be carefully co-ordinated.

Cushing's disease is caused by a tumour of the pituitary gland. Many animals over twenty have Cushing's disease, but younger ones can also have it and it is often accompanied by laminitis. With careful management many 'Cushing's' animals live comfortable, useful lives particularly if the condition is caught early. Research into a new drug, trilostane, is promising.
Symptoms include inability to cast the winter coat, curly/wavy coat, laminitis, increased thirst and urine output, susceptibility to infections, heavier parasite infestation, muscle wasting, fluctuating body weight, sweating more or less, lack of energy and abnormal oestrus cycle.

Laminitis may be caused by any condition which disturbs the blood chemistry or circulation, including digestive and metabolic problems. Drugs and antibiotics can trigger it as can stress, working on hard surfaces and carbohydrate overload. Very careful management of laminitis-prone animals can help to give them a comfortable and fairly active life.
Symptoms include the classic back-on-the-heels stance and gait (the disease can occur in any of the feet), reluctance to move or get up, raised pulse and respiration rates, strong

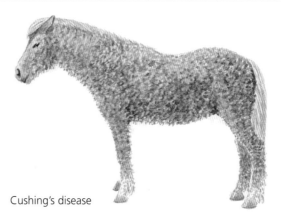

Cushing's disease

digital pulse (outside or inside of fetlock over the sesamoid bones), weight shifting and reluctance to pick up a foot because of excess weight on a painful partner.

Dental wear, broken or abscessed teeth, sharp edges ('points') and hooks make eating difficult and painful, as do overgrown teeth due to a missing partner. The molars and premolars (cheek teeth) can become worn down to the roots in old horses making eating hay, haylage and even short-chopped forage almost impossible.
Symptoms include dropping food out of mouth ('quidding'), slow eating, anxious facial expression, non-acceptance of the bit, leaving

Typical stance of the laminitic horse/pony.

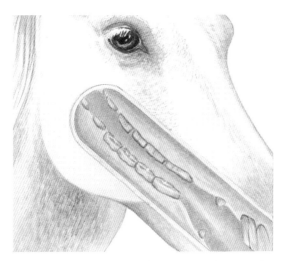

In very old horses, the teeth can wear down to the softer roots, making chewing very difficult.

feed which would normally be eaten, and undigested fibre coming out with droppings.

Osteoarthritis (degenerative joint disease – DJD) is very painful and severely restricts movement. It can occur in the neck and the back as well as in the limb joints. The cartilage which cushions the joints breaks down and pain and swelling arise as the body produces more bone to compensate.

Symptoms include pain, stiffness, lameness, weakness, hot and/or swollen joints, difficulty rising, and loss of performance.

Colic (abdominal pain) is very common in old horses and has many different causes, just a few being poor digestion, parasites, shortage of water, poisoning, insufficient fibre, particularly with high levels of concentrates, impaction, infections, gastric ulcers, drugs and antibiotics and pain-killers.
Symptoms include kicking at the belly, patchy sweating, rolling, high pulse and respiration, straddling and straining, pawing, lying on the back, leaning on the hindquarters, biting flanks, and restlessness.

Liver problems. The liver acts as a filter and as 'the food factory of the body'. It has many different functions so disease can have far-reaching effects. Disease can be caused by a lifetime of coping with stress, fat, poisons, parasites and chemicals.
Initial symptoms include jaundice (a yellowish colour of the mucous membranes), dullness and failure to thrive.

JOINT PROBLEMS

arthritic bone spur in a joint

A lot of the pain in osteoarthritis comes from bone ends grating together, due to worn or damaged cartilage.

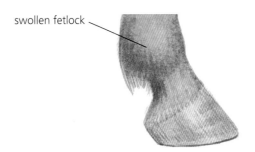

swollen fetlock

Swollen fetlocks are common in older horses with both osteoarthritis and chronic ligament damage. Such horses cannot be worked, other than at walk, on either very hard or very soft going. Horses that have jumped or raced often have both these problems.

11

Respiratory distress caused by broken wind/heaves is an allergic reaction to fungal spores and dust. Disease such as influenza or strangles may leave a horse susceptible, as can inhaled ammonia fumes from dirty stables. With good treatment and management, horses can work actively and comfortably.

Symptoms include difficulty in breathing, particularly in exhaling, coughing and loss of performance. White mucus may appear at one or both nostrils.

Broken-winded

Melanoma is a malignant tumour common in old but particularly grey equines. It is not usually life-threatening but can spread (including internally) without warning, particularly if incompletely removed during surgery.

Symptoms. The tumours are dark, smooth lumps, sometimes in clusters, found mainly under the tail but also on the sides of the face. Mainly they are unsightly but not painful and horses live with them for years. Keep a close eye on them and contact your vet if there is any change.

Worm damage can occur due to worm larvae migrating around the body and through organs; in particular the arteries and bowel wall can be severely damaged. As older horses' immune systems do not work so effectively, giving them less protection, it is essential that a proper worming programme is maintained.

Symptoms vary according to the variety of damage caused. The most common are poor condition, staring coat, colic, failure to thrive, diarrhoea and poor performance.

Cataracts may occur due to degeneration with age, following the eye disease uveitis or following a blow to the eye such as in a fall. In some cases, vision can be improved by removal of the lens.

Symptoms. The lens becomes gradually more and more cloudy, usually over a few years or more suddenly, depending on the cause.

Kidney problems. The kidneys mainly act as a filter of toxins, excess water and waste products from the blood and maintain fluid and electrolyte balance. Problems arise through dehydration, excess toxins and waste products in the blood, gut acidity, infection and other factors.

Symptoms include a change in urination and drinking habits, depression, colic, weight loss and nervousness.

Exposure ailments such as mud fever (scratches US), rain rash/scald, chapped face and muzzle, sunburn, problems caused by flies and other parasites and loss of weight due to stress and poor nutrition are more common in older horses as they are out more, yet are less able to withstand them. Good shelter and conscientious daily care are the remedies.

THE VETERAN'S ENVIRONMENT

Even today, with our supposedly more humane attitude to our horses, it is common for old horses to be 'put out to grass' until they can barely stand or dare not lie down, and then be disposed of in the fond, misplaced belief that this constitutes a 'well-earned retirement'. This is probably the exact opposite to what they really need. Like old people and other elderly creatures, they become more sensitive to extremes of weather and develop the health problems of the aged, and a life out at grass without adequate protection and care is certainly the wrong management for them.

If, like most, an old horse or pony is arthritic, it is good for him to be able to keep on the move gently, so a largely outdoor life may seem ideal. What he does not need, though, is exposure to cold, damp, mud, hot sun, flies and midges, and baked ground, all combined with inappropriate or insufficient feeding, watering, foot and dental care, clothing and health care.

It may well be better for older animals to

If old horses can have stables with the doors usually open so that they can come and go as they wish, this would be pleasing for them. Finding two friends in one stable is quite usual and no problem.

be stabled at night in winter, at least, and probably during the day in summer. The older horse will need the same (normal) precautions taken for him as when he was a working member of your family. His individual chronic problems, such as sweet itch, broken wind and laminitis, are not going to go away as he ages, and more will come.

Probably his ideal environment would be a well-drained paddock with reasonable grass growth, a roomy, solid building with a bedded-down area for him to retreat to as and when he wants, true friends and companions who will not boss or hassle him, and a close and caring human eye constantly assessing his health and demeanour.

This really would be a retirement worth having.

CHANGING DIETARY NEEDS

The main nutritional problems caused by increasing age are:

- a digestive system which naturally becomes less efficient with age;
- the effects of worm damage on the gut – wound sites produce scar tissue which does not function like normal gut tissue, so decreasing the area available for nutrient absorption; and
- teeth growing out, becoming sharp or uneven, or perhaps being broken or lost over the years.

Digestion

A poorer digestive system means, in general, that the horse's nutrients are not being processed or absorbed as effectively as formerly and, put plainly, he may well suffer from malnutrition. Because a horse, like any creature, is what he eats (or rather what he absorbs), this can result in:

- poorer overall condition and functioning
- faster ageing
- serious health problems
- earlier onset of degenerative diseases
- increased colic attacks
- lowered immune system and so increased susceptibility to diseases
- lower quality of life
- shorter life

People often put these factors down to 'getting old': they are, but the bottom line is malnutrition or even starvation. Such effects can be delayed and lessened by upgrading the horse's diet as far as nutrients are concerned, and maybe changing its physical nature to make it easier to eat.

A diet which adequately served your horse

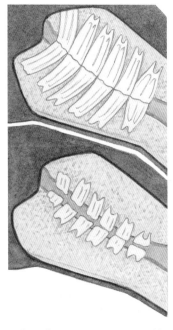

In a younger horse, the cheek (back, grinding) teeth meet evenly and are more effective at grinding up fibrous food. The roots are deep in the jaw and continue to erupt during life.

As a horse ages and the roots keep erupting, there is gradually less tooth left and the horse is left with the softer roots to grind his food. Also, the teeth may become uneven, both these factors making for imperfect grinding.

when he was younger will not do so now. Because the signs listed come on gradually, the diet will need changing gradually, too. If your horse has actually been diagnosed by your veterinary surgeon with a specific condition such as Cushing's, kidney or liver disease, the basic diet will need to deal with that, but other aspects can be factored in to improve his overall state.

Your vet should be able to help, but also do call on the (usually free) services of the qualified nutritionist at the company whose feeds you use. All good feed manufacturers have helplines, and the advice of both these experts should be blended to produce the best diet for your individual horse as time goes on.

Your horse, from about fifteen years onwards, may do better on a specific 'senior' feed and/or either a broad spectrum vitamin and mineral supplement or a specialised one. Extra oil (such as animal-feed-grade linseed oil) also benefits older horses as it is an easy way to absorb extra energy: it can also enhance their ability to make and use cholesterol-based hormones, helpful in maintaining vigour.

Parasitic worm damage

I have had success in feeding ground fenugreek seeds (a herbal remedy) to horses with worm damage. Traditionally, fenugreek is used for gastric disorders and ulceration, also to stimulate appetite and generally improve body condition. Its healing qualities make it ideal to help heal current worm damage.

Its 8 per cent oil content and 20 per cent protein content (bearing in mind that only a relatively small amount is used) and its content of calcium and vitamins A, B, C and E makes it ideal to support older horses with digestive and other problems. Three eggcup-sized scoops daily of the ground seeds might be recommended for a horse of 15.2 hh.

Teeth

The horse's teeth evolved to bite off and grind up fibre. Fibre – grass, hay, haylage and short-chopped forages – is naturally a horse's main type of food but without effective grinding teeth, and incisors to take in the food, the horse will suffer from malnutrition and all the problems it brings.

Apart from normal sharp edges and hooks, older horses develop uneven grinding surfaces on the back/cheek teeth. Eventually, as the teeth continue to erupt, the softer roots come through the gum and the horse is trying to crush fibre on grinding surfaces which may not be up to it.

In such a case, softer feeds such as high-

sugar-beet pellets

Mix high-fibre horse cubes/pellets with sugar-beet pulp and let them soak together in cold water. The resulting soft feed is tasty, nourishing and easy for horses with poor teeth to tackle.

sugar-beet shreds

horse cubes/nuts

Short-chopped forage feeds will be easier for the horse to eat than long fibre such as hay or haylage. A particularly nourishing forage for old horses with dental problems is lucerne/alfalfa.

Grated carrots are easy to eat and a favourite with most horses. They can be mixed into the feed at a rate of about 3-4kg/6-8lbs daily for a horse of 16-16.2hh.

fibre, high-nutrient cubes mixed with soaked sugar-beet pulp are easier for the horse to eat, and in fairly large quantities, under expert advice.

PREVENTATIVE MANAGEMENT

From fifteen or sixteen years of age, your horse is undeniably middle-aged and you could begin giving him 'senior horse' feeds and supplements. Watch him carefully for increased sensitivity to stress such as hard work (stiff and tired the next day, lying down more, maybe off his feed), extremes of weather (asking to come in, sheltering more) and needing more or 'richer' feed to maintain condition, strength and energy levels.

Reducing your horse or pony's physical and mental stress load can definitely improve well-being and delay the effects of ageing. Stress is a major killer in human and animal populations, both in the wild and in domesticity.

Do protect him from extremes of weather and in winter don't clip too much if at all and don't overload him with rugs as this is very uncomfortable. Feel with the flat of your hand round the base of his ears, belly, flanks and loins to check if he really feels chilly and needs a rug or two.

Veterinary help: Your veterinary surgeon can help with the management of your older horse. Vaccinations and worming should be kept up, as advised. An annual equine profile blood check can give a broad idea of the horse's general health and will indicate any areas which may need further investigation. The heart and lungs, the eyes, the joints, teeth and condition and so on will all be checked during an annual 'medical'.

Older horses often need various levels of pain-killers to remain comfortable, phenylbutazone still being popular because it is effective and cheap. Keeping the sachets in the freezer reduces the bitter taste of the

medicine and helps 'get it down'. One sign of age and the onset of osteoarthritis is the horse becoming touchy to shoe or even have his feet picked out. It may be advisable to give him 'bute for a few days before and after shoeing so that the process does not turn into a trauma. Your vet will prescribe this if necessary.

Dietary therapy: Clinical nutrition is the science of helping to treat problems by nutrition. Nutraceuticals are products which seem to be between drugs and basic feeds but are, in practice, much nearer to feeds. Discuss your horse's needs with your vet and a good nutritionist.

Management techniques

Stiffness/arthritis: Gentle exercise and freedom to wander definitely help this problem. Try to create a 'play-pen' area with shelter, water and hay where your horse is not restricted by four walls.

Broken wind: A clean-air regime is needed here – dust-free forage, feed and bedding and a well-ventilated but non-draughty stable. Once any cough has reduced, the horse should be kept in regular exercise, mainly walking at first, and kept out, with shelter, as much as possible.

Slow deterioration: Don't expect an ageing horse to be able to carry on as though he were five years younger. Reduce his workload, increase or change his diet as needed and watch for the development of conditions and diseases of old age.

Cushing's disease: The main points here are lack of energy and the need to drink more. Once the disease is under treatment these usually improve, but remember that the disease may be accompanied by laminitis. Because the winter coat is slow to shed, the horse may need clipping in spring so that his ability to lose heat through the skin and coat in warm or hot weather is not hampered.

Worn teeth: Provide soft, nutritious feed. Soaked cubes, coarse mixes and sugar beet pulp, along with grated carrots and other roots, are usually welcome. The horse may be unable to cope with long fibre such as hay and haylage so soaked, short-chopped forage should be tried. The entire ration should be weighed when dry and the horse's normal daily requirement by weight fed.

Laminitis: Expert trimming, keeping the toes short and maybe squared and rounded off, maybe with heart-bar shoes or at least frog supports, will physically help the laminitic animal greatly. Special support boots are available in the US. Do not put your horse or pony on to over-grazed, stressed grass as this can trigger the disease. Restricted, low nutrient-level grazing is best, or even a surfaced area with rationed hay/haylage, and special feeds and a supplement for laminitics are normally the answer. His weight must be kept down but he needs his nutrients.

Liver and kidney problems: These will be under the direct supervision of your vet but clinical nutrition can help greatly.

Mucking out should be done while the horse is out because of the dust, which will inevitably be raised. Open all ventilation points, rinse and brush the floor if possible, then leave it to dry, bedding down before the horse comes in.

An old herbal remedy against respiratory disease, including broken wind, is to peel and cut a couple of large onions, thread them on string or put them inside a net bag, cut side outwards, and hang them in the stable as high as possible. The few horses who will try eating them don't usually try twice! Change them weekly.

In winter, remember that your oldie will be more susceptible to cold and wet than when he was younger. On cold, windy days, wrap him up warm in a woolly exercise rug; use a waterproof one when it's raining; and don't go too far in bad weather, just far enough to keep him loosened up. Dry him off properly on return.

COMPLEMENTARY THERAPIES

As people become more and more disenchanted with conventional medicine, complementary therapies are increasing in popularity. The failures of some modern drugs, and their so-called side, or additional, effects have certainly encouraged this trend.

Complementary therapists must, in the UK, be referred by a veterinary surgeon.

Herbalism is the oldest form of medicine known, and to get the best results from the thousands of remedies for psychological and physical conditions, consult a qualified herbalist, e.g. a member of the National Institute of Medical Herbalists (in the UK) or the American Herbalists' Guild (in the USA). All herbal medicines are sourced from different parts of plants.

A form of **homeopathy** was used by the ancient Greeks, and modern homeopathy is both effective and increasingly popular. The therapy treats the patient and his or her character, lifestyle and environment, not simply the disease. Its principle is that the symptoms caused by an overdose of a substance (mainly from vegetable and mineral sources) in a healthy person or animal are those that can be cured by a small dose of that same substance in one who is sick. Choose a qualified practitioner – registered with the Society of Homeopaths in the UK, or the American Holistic Veterinary Association in the US – or a homeopathic vet.

A simple and safe therapy for owners to prescribe and administer is **flower remedies**. Available from some chemists/drug stores but also from health food shops, you can obtain a

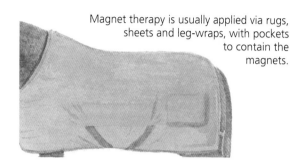

Magnet therapy is usually applied via rugs, sheets and leg-wraps, with pockets to contain the magnets.

In homeopathy, it is important not to touch the remedy as you will attract its healing element instead of your horse. The small pills can be crushed in a folded piece of paper and placed inside the horse's lip, or given on a piece of apple.

Bach Flower Remedies are the best known of the flower therapies. They are given by a dropper inside the horse's lip or added to his drinking water.

Horses have been treating themselves for millions of years by means of natural 'herbalism'. Dandelions, shown here, are famously used as a diuretic, also a mild laxative, general tonic and liver remedy, and for rheumatism.

leaflet telling you how to decide what your horse needs. They are made from flowers and the system is closely related to homeopathy.

Reiki (hands-on healing) involves sending healing energies through the hands, but it can also be sent from a distance. The energy sent by the practitioner is said to be attracted to wherever it is needed in the body.

Aromatherapy relies on the scent of beneficial essential oils derived from plants. Scents are minute particles carried on the air which are breathed in and dissolve in the moisture of the airways. A practitioner can devise a particular blend for specific personalities and physical conditions.

Magnet therapy is used to treat stiffness, injuries and other disorders. Some feel that ordinary magnets have little effect and that only electrically pulsed magnetic therapy is worthwhile. There are at least three accepted theories as to how it helps, but help it certainly seems to.

Physiotherapy is a recognised range of treatments performed by qualified personnel comprising massage, manipulation, stretching, specialised machines, hydrotherapy, remedial exercise and the application of heat and/or cold. **Sports** or **therapeutic massage** is enjoyed by most horses and really helps them to feel rejuvenated! It enhances circulation, loosens up muscles and other soft tissues and increases mobility and elasticity.

Osteopathy and **chiropractic** work on the skeleton and spine respectively. The principle

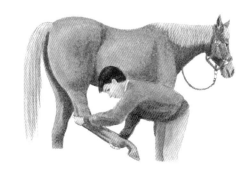

Careful stretching can help old horses retain mobility and suppleness but expert advice and instruction must be taken, particularly for horses with physical problems such as osteoarthritis or old injuries.

Hand rubbing is an old grooms' speciality. Using the hands and forearms, it is soothing and invigorating to the horse, and is a light form of beneficial massage of the skin and superficial muscles.

is that skeletal misalignments cause nerve pressure and encourage muscle spasms, affecting mobility and health. Skilful manipulation aims to release spasms and remove the painful 'pulling' effect on bones and joints.

Shiatsu is related to acupuncture but uses mainly finger pressure instead of needles. It is believed that disturbances of the body's energy or life force show as physical or psychological disorders. Shiatsu aims to rebalance the flow of energy by pressure on various points and meridians or directions along which the energy flows. It is a gentle and effective therapy.

19

TEACHING AN OLDER HORSE NEW TRICKS

Horses have survived for millions of years in the wild and with man because they are extremely adaptable animals. They adapt to new homes, new owners with different ways and beliefs, and new friends. They learn quickly if well taught, so there is no need for the commonly held belief that horses' ways and mentalities are set in stone. They are not.

It could be a major trauma for a horse to change home, owner, diet, surroundings, friends and work all at once, but it happens regularly and it is surprising how well horses do adapt if made to feel secure. As always, the diet must be changed gradually so some of his old feed should be procured for mixing in at first. The normal careful introductions should be made to new friends, and every effort should be made to stable the newcomer next to a horse with whom he is making friends, to increase his security and help him to settle. To force horses to exist away from friends and, certainly, near an enemy, is bad

Hunters from galloping countries can go on to less demanding hunting and, like most horses, enjoy being a personal or family hack. I have known several, though, who never really quite settled without the excitement of the chase.

Because dressage is an integral part of eventing, retiring event horses often take to competitive dressage as they are already used to it.

horsemastership.

It often does a new arrival good to have at least a few days off to become familiar with his new colleagues, other animals and humans. When a horse has been fighting fit and is going to a less demanding regime, a longer break is a good plan.

Getting old is also a human concept. The horse has no idea how old he is or how long he probably has left to live. His body dictates to him how he feels, what he feels he can do and what he wants to do. A horse who has grazed and played freely all his life will know when he's starting to feel stiffer, maybe in pain, and will obviously know that getting his head down to eat, galloping and kicking around, and getting down to roll, rolling itself and getting up again are all much more uncomfortable and difficult. He will then reduce these activities.

A working, performance horse, say a show-jumper or hunter, similarly, will know when fences of a certain height and spread are too big a challenge, but will still be happy to jump something lower and shallower. A horse whose job has involved fast and/or sustained galloping, such as a racehorse or an eventer,

First impressions are as important to horses as to us. Have his stable cleaned out and disinfected to remove other horse smells as much as possible, plenty of fresh bedding, water and hay or haylage, ideally from his former home. Do not stable him next to a horse you know to be an 'alpha' type unless it is also usually friendly towards other horses.

may still be happy to go for as fast or as long as he can now, but that will be slower and not so far as previously.

In short, he is winding down a bit.

Many older horses move quite successfully from one career to another. I well remember a High School stallion some years ago who, according to his perceptive and very skilled owner, decided that he did not want the indignity of being sat upon any more. It seems that he did not have a back problem because he bucked, played and rolled in his field just as much as before. His owner decided to keep to High School work on long reins and for many more years the pair gave entertaining, enthusiastic and educational displays in this art.

Ex-racehorses often turn out to be very versatile for those who are sensitive enough to see through to the Thoroughbred spirit and have the tact to handle this breed.

WE USED TO BE FRIENDS – HERD STATUS

Horses have phenomenal memories so must remember places, people and animals. My first horse showed no recognition of his breeder during a visit, or his first livery yard five years after moving. My former show-jumper went to a familiar venue for a flatwork demonstration, and spent the evening on pins waiting for the bell to start her round!

Newcomers to a yard must feel strange and their owners should do everything possible to make them feel secure and cared for.

One of the sad things often noticed about old horses is their changing relationship with the other members of their herd. In the wild, younger, stronger animals try to strengthen their positions in the herd and the weaker ones are pushed away.

This sort of thing can be quite distressing to old animals. Their reducing social status can be hard to accept but they find that they are physically and mentally unable to fight off a challenge.

In practice, older horses, once they start weakening, are often to be found on the margins of their herd and/or the subjects of unwelcome attention. Other animals who are younger and stronger and who are trying to cement their position and social acceptance in the herd may prevent the old horse coming to his friends, and vice versa. In the wild, such rejection can end up with the older horse being picked off by predators. In domesticity, it can result in a lack of contentment, which alone is enough to prevent the horse thriving.

Your old horse or pony should be put with, say, one or more non-threatening friends and watched carefully for the formation of social mores which indicate whether or not the horse is being fully accepted. Bullying and harassment are the very last things an old horse needs in addition to feeling his age.

If horses are given bucket feeds in the field or shelter, it may be wiser and kinder to feed the old horse separately so he can eat his ration in peace and get his vital, specialised nutrients: this will help to maintain his well-being which, in turn, will help him to retain his position in his herd. Being seen by the others to receive any extra care from humans also does this.

Although it may not be so obvious as shown here, take time frequently to watch your horse's relationship with his field mates. Even the subtlest signs that he or she is being excluded can be a indication that action, on your part, must be taken to look after your horse's interests.

OBEDIENCE AND THE OLDER EQUINE

Obedience can be a tricky topic. If you have an old horse with whom you have a close relationship, even if that relationship has not lasted long, you are likely to be less strict with him than with other horses.

It is often the case that 'disobedience' or lack of co-operation in older horses may be the only way that they can tell us that what we are asking is no longer within their capabilities and they are objecting because (a) they know that they just cannot do what we are asking any more, or (b) it causes them pain, discomfort or costs just too much effort, in their physically deteriorating condition.

This is certainly a test of your skill as a horsemaster – that old-fashioned word which does not particularly mean 'master of horses' but carer of, and for, horses. Most people attuned to horses can tell when a horse is genuinely past what we are asking or is 'pulling the wool'. In general I think that it is fine to let older horses take reasonable liberties with us. Most of them know how far to go and not many horses will start to hurt humans because of this.

It is often the case that an older horse, like older people, may eventually feel that he has had enough of a particular activity, practice, routine or whatever and, in a case like that, I feel that it is good horsemastership to accept his decision and go along with him. Most horse people, though, would probably draw the line at a horse who started napping at the yard gate, ripping his rugs or shying out hacking, and new behaviours like these should certainly be checked up on.

If your horse starts taking charge of you rather than taking care of you (if that has been his way), it normally only takes a few sharp words with a wise veteran to let him know he has crossed the line. Although he may feign disdain at his telling off he does know where both of you stand.

Refusing fences can be a sign that the older horse is sick of his job and needs a change, or is in pain or discomfort. Or, if an older horse has changed homes, the new rider may be causing the problem.

A traffic-safe old horse can be worth his weight in gold. If his trustworthy behaviour starts to change, suspect deteriorating eyesight or hearing and call the vet.

'I know what you want but I don't feel like it today.' If this is like your oldster, can you decide whether to persist or give him the benefit of the doubt? If the latter, are you encouraging him to be hard to catch? Is he the type to take advantage of your 'giving in', or honest enough to co-operate another day? Only you can decide!

'SUIT ACTIVE PENSIONER'

What sorts of job can you expect older horses to do? Because 'older' horses can range from about fifteen to twenty-five and more, it does very much depend on their actual physical condition, any chronic problems from previous careers, attitude and natural likes and talents.

We can safely say that late-teenagers would not be suited to high-level eventing, steeplechasing, point-to-pointing (although I once bought as a hack a nineteen-year-old whose owner was preparing him for another season), hard hunting in a fast country, 100-mile races – you get the picture. Of course, there are bound to be exceptions, but all oldies should not be expected to live up to their example.

The jobs which ideally suit older horses, depending on their abilities and health, are hacking, moderate hunting, organised pleasure rides, dressage, show-jumping at lower heights than formerly, veteran show classes and others such as Family Horse or Pony, Handy Hunter, combined training (dressage and show-jumping), private or pleasure driving – indeed anything which is easily within the horse or pony's capabilities, easily being the operative word.

Jobs which the horse enjoys actually help to delay the ageing process by keeping him fit without stress and feeling still part of things. This is the important point. You really do have to be a good judge of a horse's mind and

Hacking out gently or more actively, depending on what the horse can do, is a good and enjoyable way of keeping an old horse exercised and on the move. Consider any ailments he may have, though. For instance, if he has arthritis he should probably only walk on roads to prevent concussion; if chronic ligament damage and weakness are his problem, conversely, soft or deep going will be uncomfortable for him.

body to know when he is truly enjoying what he does and can do it, when he enjoys what he does but can no longer do it, and when he just doesn't enjoy it any more.

Older horses can, of course, have several changes of job and career, going gradually and gently down the scale of demand. For example, an eventer could go from eventing to show-jumping and hunting, then to organised pleasure rides and dressage and finally to hacking. Outgrown children's ponies are prime candidates for becoming driving ponies for the adults of the family. Even being a companion in retirement to another horse is a valuable and suitable job, of course, provided the companion is not treated like a second-class citizen.

With good care, consideration and a perceptive eye, you should be able to give yourself and your old horse several more happy years together.

Euthanasia is something many owners don't want to face but, when the need arises, is the most important thing we can do for our horses. Horses may be shot with a humane killer or put down with a drug specially for euthanasia – not an overdose of anaesthetic.